The Illustrated Book of
Ballet Stories

Aurora and her prince
celebrate their wedding in
The Sleeping Beauty

The Illustrated Book of
Ballet Stories

Stories written by
Barbara Newman

Illustrated by
Gill Tomblin

With an Introduction by
Darcey Bussell

LONDON, NEW YORK, MUNICH,
MELBOURNE, and DELHI

Stories written by Barbara Newman
Illustrated by Gill Tomblin
Project editor Lorrie Mack
Art editor Laura Roberts

Publishing manager Susan Leonard
Managing art editor Clare Shedden
Jacket designer Karen Shooter
Jacket editor Carrie Love
Jacket copywriter Adam Powley
Picture researcher Sarah Pownall
Picture librarian Sarah Mills
Production Alison Lenane
DTP designer Almudena Díaz

First published in Great Britain in 1997
This revised edition published in 2005 by
Dorling Kindersley Limited
80 Strand, London WC2R ORL

A Penguin Company

2 4 6 8 10 9 7 5 3 1

Copyright © 2005 Dorling Kindersley Limited, London

A CIP catalogue record for this book
is available from the British Library.

ISBN 1-4053-1030-8

Colour reproduction by Colourscan, Singapore
Printed and bound in China by L-Rex.

Discover more at
www.dk.com

Contents

CD Contents

 When this star symbol appears in the stories, it indicates where the musical selections fall in each ballet. The number in the star is the number of the corresponding CD track.

Introduction

Welcome to the timeless world of ballet. I never tire of performing the classical ballets, which combine wonderful fairy-tale stories with magical music, and I have enjoyed dancing in all five of the ballets featured in this book.

If I had to choose a favourite ballet, it would be *Swan Lake*. Not only was it my first classical ballet, performed at the age of 20, but I was also fortunate enough to receive coaching from Margot Fonteyn. In this ballet, it is always a challenge to dance the very different characters of Odette and Odile in one evening. I find that the mood of the music brings out the contrast between the White Swan and the Black Swan and helps to define these roles.

All the ballets described in this book are more than a hundred years old. I am sure they will continue to weave their magic and go on entertaining for many more years. I hope you will enjoy them as much as I do.

PREPARING FOR A PERFORMANCE
Classical ballets are known for their strenuous and technical choreography. In order to feel confident performing these ballets, a dancer must devote a lot of rehearsal time to them. This makes it possible to build up the stamina and strength to enjoy dancing these roles.

ODETTE/ODILE IN *SWAN LAKE*

When I first performed *Swan Lake*, I gained most enjoyment from dancing the Black Swan (Odile), given the evil and seductive power that she has. I now find that the quieter strength and the lyrical nature of the White Swan (Odette) is just as exciting to portray.

MY ROLE MODEL

I have tried to incorporate the best work of many great dancers into my performances. However, if there is one quality I admire most, it is the ability to bring a magic and glow to the stage in every ballet. Nobody did this better than Margot Fonteyn.

DANCING PARTNERS

Working with a partner requires complete trust. To be an excellent partner you must have strength, confidence, and the ability to know both your partner's role and your own. This allows the most complex movements to look graceful and simple.

GISELLE

Giselle has to change from a young country girl, carefree and happy with life, to a broken-hearted spirit in just one interval. I love the challenge of this choreography; it offers an unusually wide range of styles, to suit earthy peasants and wispy spirits.

THE SLEEPING BEAUTY

This is one of the most strenuous ballets for the female lead. Knowing what you have to achieve creates such pressure that your nerves nearly stop you from making your first entrance. After the difficult Rose Adagio in the birthday scene, however, the weight lifts and you can enjoy the rest of the performance.

Soft shoes

*Anchoring elastic
is stitched here.*

PRACTICE SHOES
Boys and girls both wear soft ballet shoes for class. Elastic strips keep the shoes on, and a thin cord threaded around the top pulls tight to create a neat fit. The ends are tied in a small bow and tucked away.

Satin ribbons keep pointe shoes in place.

ON YOUR TOES
For performances, rehearsals, and some classes, girls wear shoes with stiffened (called blocked) toes so they can dance on pointe. Unless these are part of a special costume, they are made of pink satin.

PERSONAL TOUCH
Pointe shoes should give support and protection, yet allow dancers to "feel" the floor. Darning the toes helps them to grip. Professional dancers have their pointe shoes custom made.

8

Ballet basics

Ballet classes are the same everywhere. They are usually taught in mirrored studios that have springy floors and handrails called *barres*, which are either fixed to the wall or freestanding. Dancers wear practice clothes that are comfortable but close-fitting so their bodies can be seen clearly. Hair is neat, and jewellery is left in the changing room so it can't catch, scratch, or distract. Because ballet was developed in France, the French language is still used to teach and describe it all over the world.

Elbows and wrists are gently rounded.

Hair is tied back and pinned neatly.

Fingers are soft and graceful, and continue the line of the arm.

Boys wear cotton T-shirts.

Leotards fit snugly to define the body.

Designed for rehearsals and partnering classes, practice tutus look and feel like real costumes.

For class, most boys wear black tights – with or without feet.

Tights were originally woven from cotton or silk, but modern ones are made from stretchy, washable synthetics.

Footless tights are worn with socks. Cotton ones absorb sweat and let skin breathe.

Pointe shoes are stiffened with glue at the toes. Some dancers soften new shoes by banging them on a hard surface.

Boys' practice shoes can be white or black.

Positions of the arms and feet

ARMS: The placement of the arms is vital in classical ballet. Arms not only form graceful lines and shapes, they also provide balance, support, and momentum.

FIRST POSITION The arms make an oval shape in front of the body at waist level.

When the oval is lowered toward the thighs, the position is called bras bas *(low arms).*

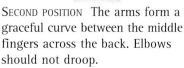

SECOND POSITION The arms form a graceful curve between the middle fingers across the back. Elbows should not droop.

There should be no sharp angles at the elbows or wrists.

Shoulders are always relaxed and down.

THIRD POSITION One arm is curved to the side as in second position, and the other is curved in front, as in first.

FOURTH POSITION Here, one arm is curved to the side and the other one forms a curve above, and just in front of, the face.

FIFTH POSITION The arms form an oval above the head, and slightly in front. The hands are about a face-width apart.

FEET: All exercises and steps begin from one of the five basic positions of the feet. In each one, the legs are turned out from the hips so the knees and feet face sideways.

FIRST POSITION Forming a straight line, the feet are touching at the heels with the toes pointing in opposite directions.

SECOND POSITION The feet form the same line as they do in first position, but the heels are the length of one foot apart.

THIRD POSITION Parallel to one another, the feet are aligned so the heel of the front foot touches the middle of the back one.

FOURTH POSITION The feet are parallel to one another so that one is exactly in front of the other and the length of one foot apart.

FIFTH POSITION The feet are lined up and fully crossed so the toe of one touches the heel of the other.

BEND AND STRETCH

Pliés stretch and warm muscles and give movements spring and bounce. *Plié* means bend or fold; in a *demi-plié* (half bend), the heels stay on the floor and the knees bend half-way. In a *grand plié* (full bend), the thighs are parallel with the floor and the heels are raised.

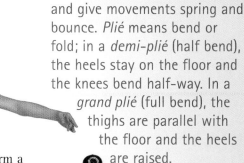

Demi-plié   *Grand plié*

TONE AND STRENGTHEN

Battement tendu (stretched beating) tones, stretches, and strengthens legs and feet. It involves keeping both legs straight and sliding one away from the other and back again, pointing the toes each time. Like most exercises, it is done to the front, the side, the back, and the side again: in the rough shape of a cross, or *en croix*.

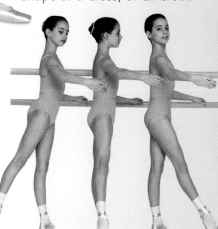

Dancers do each exercise with one leg, then turn around to repeat it with the other.

9

The Sleeping Beauty

THE SLEEPING BEAUTY is based on a 17th-century fairy tale by Charles Perrault. Marius Petipa created the choreography and contributed to the story's adaptation, and Peter Ilyich Tchaikovsky composed the music – the second of his three great ballet scores – between *Swan Lake* and *The Nutcracker*. The first performance was given by the Imperial Ballet at the Maryinsky Theater, St Petersburg, in 1890. *The Sleeping Beauty* has a Prologue followed by three acts.

The Sleeping Beauty

At the christening

★ ONCE UPON A TIME a princess was born in a kingdom far away. The king and queen named their daughter Aurora, and they invited all the fairies of the kingdom to attend her royal christening at the palace.

One by one the fairies arrived in the great hall to present their splendid gifts to the baby and her proud parents. But just as the Lilac Fairy approached the cradle, black shadows filled the room and the castle shook with thunder. An uninvited guest, the evil fairy Carabosse, swept into the hall in a billowing cloud of smoke. "Why was I not invited to the christening?" she screeched at the quaking king and queen. "I will have my revenge for this cruel insult. I, too, will give your precious daughter a gift."

A horrible curse leapt from her mouth. "Aurora will grow into a beautiful girl," Carabosse sneered, "but one day she will prick her finger on something sharp. And the moment she pricks her finger, she will die".

THE FACE OF CARABOSSE

In this Royal Ballet production, the part of the evil fairy is played by ballerina Zenaida Yanowsky. Often, the role is taken by an older, character dancer – sometimes a man in a long skirt, heavy make-up, and a wig. The term "character" refers to roles where the dancer moves in a natural way rather than performing ballet steps.

VERSATILE ARTIST

At the ballet's premiere in 1890, both the character role of Carabosse and the technically difficult part of the Bluebird were played by Italian dancer and mime artist Enrico Ceccetti. Ceccetti was also a great teacher, and the teaching system he developed is still in use all over the world.

Carabosse appears from nowhere in her rumbling black coach. Her ghastly face glows with anger and evil.

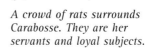

A crowd of rats surrounds Carabosse. They are her servants and loyal subjects.

The sobbing queen begged Carabosse to change her mind, but the evil fairy only laughed in her face. Luckily, the Lilac Fairy had not yet given the baby her gift of wisdom. Stepping forward, she silenced Carabosse's hideous cackling with a sweet spell of her own.

"Here is my gift," she said gently. "Aurora will indeed grow up, prick her finger, and collapse. But she will not die. Instead she will fall into a deep sleep that will last until a handsome prince kisses her. Only then will the spell be broken."

Overpowered by the Lilac Fairy's loving gift, Carabosse vanished from the scene with a furious hiss. The hall grew bright again as the guests clustered around the cradle to admire the baby princess.

PAST GLORIES
In 1999, the Kirov Ballet launched a new production of *The Sleeping Beauty* with designs based on those of the first performance. Worn here by Veronika Part, the Lilac Fairy's costume suggests that her original steps were very different from the intricate pointe work performed today.

Aurora's nursemaid watches over her cradle.

Attendant fairies bless the baby with gifts and dancing.

The Lilac Fairy graces the gathering with her elegance.

To express sleep, dancers tilt their head and form a pillow with their arms.

STORIES WITHOUT WORDS
The traditional language of mime allows dancers to "speak" to each other – and to give details of the story – without making a sound. Nineteenth-century audiences would have been familiar with all the basic mime gestures.

The Sleeping Beauty
Aurora's birthday party

MUSICAL FESTIVITIES
For the party, the palace gardens are decorated with flowers. Aurora's friends celebrate with a graceful waltz, which is sometimes called the Garland Dance. In this version, Gaylene Cummerfield and Matthew Donnelly of the Australian Ballet follow its familiar and much-loved tune.

THE YEARS PASSED, and Aurora grew into a lovely girl under her parents' watchful care. When Carabosse had uttered her wicked curse, the king issued a decree to protect Aurora. He banished every sharp object from the palace grounds, so no knife or needle could ever harm her.

⭐ One summer afternoon, all Aurora's friends gathered in the royal gardens to celebrate her sixteenth birthday. To their amazement, they noticed three old women knitting busily in the sun. "Grab them," the courtiers cried. "Stop that at once," the guards shouted. But when the queen took pity on the old women, the king forgave them.

"Where's my birthday girl?" the king laughed, and at last Aurora appeared, looking as radiant as a sunbeam. Four dashing princes had travelled from distant kingdoms in the hope of marrying her. Dazzled by her beauty and charm, they took turns flattering her and offered roses and compliments along with their hearts and kingdoms.

COURTSHIP DANCE
Four suitors come to Aurora's party in the hope of winning her hand; each one brings flowers and she receives them all in turn. This dance, known as the Rose Adagio, is a great test of strength and skill for the ballerina – here, The Royal Ballet's Darcey Bussell.

The hopeful suitors cannot take their eyes off the graceful princess.

Aurora dances with all four of the visiting princes, twirling lightly from one to another.

Darting among them with a sweet smile, Aurora nearly collided with a shrivelled crone, who handed her a posy of fresh flowers concealing a shiny spindle. "Happy birthday, my dear," she croaked. Unaware of any danger, Aurora waved the posy gaily over her head and teasingly dodged everyone who tried to snatch it away.

Suddenly, the spindle's sharp tip pierced her finger. Crying out with surprise, Aurora spun dizzily between her horrified guests and then crumpled to the ground. The crone tossed back her black hood and revealed her identity – it was Carabosse. With a triumphant cackle she disappeared in a flash of lightning.

As the queen bent over her child, the Lilac Fairy rose magically from the babble and confusion. "Carry Aurora inside," she said. "She is not dead. Remember, she is only sleeping." With her words, vines began to twist around the marble columns. A veil of leaves drifted over the palace walls, and everyone inside fell asleep.

BIRTHDAY PRESENT
These bright blooms conceal the poisoned spindle described in the evil fairy's curse. A spindle is a old-fashioned hand tool used for twisting yarn into thread on a spinning wheel. For the Stuttgart Ballet, Julia Krämer is Aurora and Ivan Cavallari plays Carabosse.

Carabosse chortles with glee at the terrible result of her wicked curse.

When the king sees his daughter stretched out before him, he is sure she is dead.

Surprised by its sharp point, Aurora drops the spindle to the ground.

THE CURSE TAKES HOLD
As soon as the spindle pricks her finger, Aurora begins to swoon. Soon, she, and the rest of the court, will fall into a deep, deep sleep that lasts for one hundred years. In this staging by the National Opera of Ukraine, Kiev, Aurora is danced by Anna Dorsh.

15

DRESSING THE STAGE
Most ballet costumes are structured so that dancers can move easily and their bodies can be seen. Those that are made for background characters, however, are intended more for stage decoration. This costume for Act 2 was created by Russian painter and designer Léon Bakst (1866-1924).

The Sleeping Beauty
A vision appears

Aurora slept undisturbed in the highest turret of the palace for one hundred years. Songbirds nested in the tangled briars and thick moss carpeted the stone stairs, and still no one came to break the spell.

Meanwhile, in a forest many miles away, a young prince, Florimund, went hunting one day with his friends. Everyone could see that the handsome prince was bored with the hunting and only joined in so he would not offend his guests.

"Perhaps you would prefer a game of hide and seek?" his partner suggested cheerfully. But the prince wanted only to be left alone with his thoughts. "Let the royal hunt proceed without me," he finally commanded, dismissing his puzzled friends with a flourish.

Suddenly a voice echoed like rustling leaves in the stillness. "Why are you so unhappy?" asked the Lilac Fairy. Startled, Florimund bowed low before the gracious creature who addressed him.

"I don't know why," he admitted sadly.

"I will show you something wonderful that will lift your spirits. Look," she urged.

A TOUCH OF REALITY

Every new revival of this beloved ballet is slightly different, and each one is made to fit a specific stage. If there is enough room, real musicians in full costume may join the hunting scene, and play their instruments in front of the audience.

Some of the courtiers ride off to hunt in another part of the forest.

Florimund pays no attention to his elegant partner.

16

The prince raised his downcast eyes and saw a shimmering vision of Aurora, as light as a cloud.

"How beautiful she is," he exclaimed, and all at once the vision stood on the forest floor, surrounded by tiny fairies. The prince tiptoed nearer and stretched out his hand to touch her. Each time he came closer, the fairies flew between them. But at last, for a single instant, he held the vision in his arms. The next instant, she was gone.

"Oh, no," he cried. "Please bring her back. I love her."

"If you love her," the Lilac Fairy answered, "you must go to her yourself and tell her so".

"I would go anywhere to find that princess again," Florimund declared bravely. So the Lilac Fairy led him across the fields and over the silvery seas to the palace where Aurora lay dreaming.

AURORA REVEALED
In the Kirov Ballet's reconstruction, the Lilac Fairy (Daria Pavlenko) presents Aurora (Jenne Ayupova) to the prince (Anton Korsakov) as a vision, balanced daintily in *arabesque* on a garlanded half shell.

When the Lilac Fairy waves her shining wand, a vision of Aurora appears among the dark branches.

MIME: SEE
To express see, the dancer's pointed index fingers are placed just below the eyes, then moved down and away from the face.

Their long voyage brings them to Aurora's palace.

Without hesitating, the prince boards the Lilac Fairy's boat.

The Sleeping Beauty
The awakening

Musical note

Tchaikovsky felt powerfully drawn to the original Perrault fairy tale. "The subject is so poetic, so inspiring to composition, that I am captivated by it," he wrote to a close friend.

THE SHADOWY PALACE walls towered over the Lilac Fairy's boat like a sleeping giant. Prince Florimund's heart pounded with excitement and fear as he pushed open the heavy, rusting gates and crossed the courtyard. Inside the cracked oaken door, the king's guards lay in snoring heaps.

The hallways were dark as caves. Florimund could hear nothing but the creaking floorboards under his feet and the rattle of the wind in the tall towers. The Lilac Fairy glided along beside him, lighting his way with the glow of her magical presence.

THE KISS

When Prince Florimund (Johan Kobborg) discovers Princess Aurora (Alina Cojocaru) fast asleep, he kisses her lovingly and breaks the curse of Carabosse. This scene is from the Royal Ballet production of *The Sleeping Beauty*.

WHAT'S IN A NAME?

In modern versions of the ballet, the prince is usually called Florimund; in the original production, he was Desiré. In an obscure opera of the tale, he was Prince Lindor, while the Disney cartoon calls him Prince Phillip. In most tellings of the fairy tale, however, he is simply "the prince".

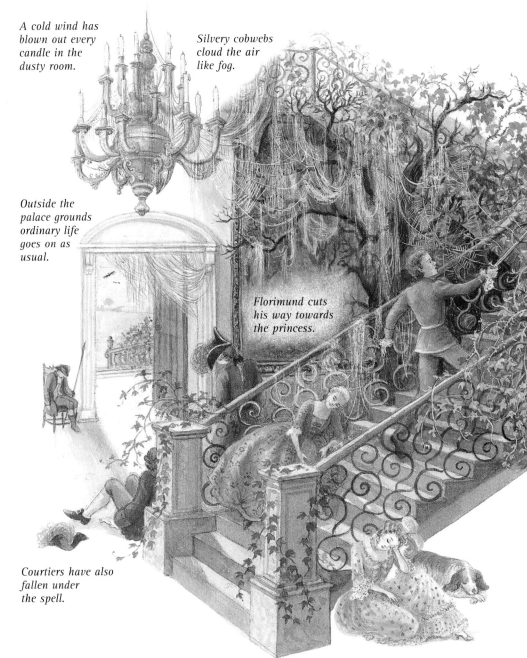

A cold wind has blown out every candle in the dusty room.

Silvery cobwebs cloud the air like fog.

Outside the palace grounds ordinary life goes on as usual.

Florimund cuts his way towards the princess.

Courtiers have also fallen under the spell.

Drawing his sword, Florimund bounded up the palace stairs, slashing at the knotted vines to clear a path. The dust stung his eyes and filled his throat. Spiders scurried over his hands, and mice skittered under his feet, but he climbed higher and higher, guided by the Lilac Fairy.

When he reached the topmost tower, he found Aurora stretched out on the silken bed, still as a corpse.

"She's dead," he groaned. "What shall I do?"

"She's not dead," promised the Lilac Fairy. "Think back. You must let her know you love her."

Florimund paused for a second, then leaned down and kissed Aurora tenderly. Her eyes fluttered open and, taking his hand, she sat up and thanked him with a smile as bright as a star.

Down in the throne room, the king and queen were brushing the cobwebs off each other's crown. As they rose to their feet, Aurora burst into the room, pulling Florimund behind her.

"Here is the prince who broke the spell," she announced, "and he is the prince I choose for my husband."

When dancers use mime, their legs can be in any position.

Listen

Think

MIME: LISTEN AND THINK
The boy demonstrates the mime gesture for listen by tapping his middle fingers lightly to his ears. The girl mimes think by tapping the first two fingers of one hand twice against her temple.

The prince discovers Aurora, who is the vision he saw in the forest.

Aurora's love for the prince fills her with happiness and hope.

Florimund takes Aurora in his arms and vows never to let her go.

DREAM LOVER
When Aurora is awakened by her Prince, they express their joy in a romantic pas de deux. Berenice Coppieters and Chris Roelandt star in this modern *Beauty* by Les Ballets de Monte Carlo.

The Sleeping Beauty
The wedding

IN A TWINKLING, one hundred years of dust was swept away. The palace was polished until it shone, and pastry cooks baked dozens of delicious cakes while scurrying footmen filled all the rooms with fragrant wild roses and sprays of lilac.

On the day of Aurora's wedding to Florimund, sunlight as golden as honey flooded the banquet hall. Royal guests came from far and wide to wish the bride and groom long life and good fortune. Aurora herself invited her closest friends from childhood, who she introduced to her new husband one by one.

First the fluffy White Cat picked her way across the floor. With every step she glanced over her shoulder and winked at Puss in Boots, who bounded after her and scratched her back with his tickling paws.

SOARING BLUEBIRD
The brief dance for the Bluebird is one of the most difficult male solos in ballet. It requires high leaps, quick turns, and fluttering beats in which the feet crisscross many times in mid-air. This high-flying performance is by the Kirov Ballet's Dmitry Seminov.

HUNGRY AS A WOLF
Suspended mid-pounce, Amar Dhaliwal portrays a terrifying Wolf that threatens Red Riding Hood in this Canadian production mounted by the Royal Winnipeg Ballet.

The hungry Wolf tries to catch Little Red Riding Hood and carry her away.

The Bluebird flies through his dizzying solo.

Princess Florine listens for the Bluebird, who will guide her away from her enchanter.

Four of the smallest pages carrying slim, gilded branches created a forest for Little Red Riding Hood. Licking his lips hungrily, the Wolf chased her through the trees. Then he pounced on her from behind, slung her over his shoulder, and loped off with a growl.

Next a pair of Bluebirds swooped and dipped above the guests' heads. One was really the enchanted Princess Florine, and the other was teaching her how to fly so she could escape from her enchanter. Their sparkling plumage reflected the sun as they soared in and out through the open windows.

Finally, Princess Aurora and Prince Florimund crowned the wedding celebration by declaring their love for each other.

"I love you," murmured Aurora. She was a little shy of speaking in front of so many people.

"I love you even more," answered Florimund.

The Lilac Fairy hovered over their heads, saying "Sharing your love and trust, you will surely live happily ever after".

FLYING FUR
When dancers portray animals, they often wear headdresses. These can be very hot, and they restrict vision and even breathing – especially during a taxing solo. Here, Lucille Robert and Patrice Lasserre (Ballet du Capitole de Toulouse) are the White Cat and Puss in Boots.

SUBTLE SUPPORT
To end their dance, Aurora dives into Florimund's arms. He supports her on one thigh while she anchors her legs under his arm. Since her body curves as if she were swimming under water, the pose is called a "fish dive". This one is executed by Roberta Durlai and Dimitri Rodikov (Vienna Festival Ballet).

Cooks from the royal kitchen have baked a beautiful wedding cake.

Hundreds of roses decorate the palace for this special day.

The king and queen are delighted at the happy match.

The Russian guests tumble into a lively folk dance.

The White Cat and Puss in Boots perform a pas de chat (meaning "step of the cat").

When the fairy-tale creatures finish their entertainment, Aurora and Florimund proclaim their love for each other.

21

Giselle

ɪɴSPIRED BY AN OLD GERMAN LEGEND set in the Rhine Valley, the romantic story of *Giselle* was written by Théophile Gautier and Vernoy de Saint-Georges. Jean Coralli and Jules Perrot choreographed the ballet, and Adolphe Adam composed the music. The first performance of *Giselle* was given at the Opéra in Paris in June 1841. Since then, it has remained popular with ballet audiences, and is now danced by nearly every classical company in the world.

Giselle

In the village

LONG AGO IN A VILLAGE FAR AWAY, a pretty girl named Giselle lived with her mother Berthe in a thatched cottage. She was the happiest girl in the village, because she was madly in love with two things. One was dancing and the other was a boy, a newcomer to the village, named Loys. Giselle felt sure he loved her in return.

Her devotion to Loys greatly annoyed Hilarion, the local gamekeeper, because he loved Giselle too. However, neither of them knew that Loys was actually a count in disguise. He had noticed Giselle in the fields one day and come to the village to win her affection, hiding his true name and identity.

One morning he coaxed her away from her chores and flattered her until she blushed pink.

HE LOVES ME NOT
Plucking daisy petals in the traditional game, Giselle looks for reassurance of Loys' love. She gets a worrying answer, but she chooses to ignore it. Alina Cojocaru and Johan Kobborg lead this Royal Ballet performance.

The dancer's arms should frame the face without covering it.

MIME: DANCE
To express dance, performers raise their softly curved arms over their head, then circle their hands around each other smoothly and widely. This mime gesture, which appears several times in *Giselle*, is one of most widely used in ballet.

Inside his cottage, Loys hides his sword and cloak.

Berthe worries that Giselle will exhaust herself by dancing.

Daisies grow wild around the cottage.

24

☆₃ "Do you really love me?" she asked. "Honestly?"

"Of course I do. You have my promise," he answered. ☆₄

"Catch me if you can," giggled Giselle, dodging his embrace playfully, but Loys caught up with her. ☆₅ Tucking her arm through his, he led her and all her friends into a merry dance.

Hilarion could not bear to watch. "What about me?" he protested.

Knowing her response would hurt his feelings, Giselle said nothing, but her glowing eyes spoke for her. She would gladly have danced with Loys forever.

☆₆ She was disappointed when her mother came bustling into the clearing and took charge. "Be careful," Berthe warned. "Too much dancing will make you ill. The woods are full of the dreadful spirits of girls just like you who could not stop dancing even after they died."

As Giselle threw Loys a kiss and skipped indoors, Hilarion suddenly had an idea. When he was quite alone, he drew his dagger, picked the lock on Loys' cottage and sneaked inside.

GOLDEN OPPORTUNITY

A featured dance like the Peasant pas de deux gives promising young artists a chance to step out of the corps de ballet and appear in the spotlight as soloists. In some modern productions, the duet becomes a pas de six. Here, Alexander Saitsev of the Stuttgart Ballet performs the male solo.

Loys' cottage is so simple that no one suspects his real identity.

The nobles who live in the distant castle seldom visit the vineyards.

Ignoring her mother's advice, Giselle dances with Loys as often as she can.

Hilarion breaks into Loys' cottage, to satisfy his curiosity about the stranger.

Charmed by Giselle's gaiety, Loys is happy to remain in disguise.

ROMANCE AND FANTASY

When *Giselle* was created in the middle of the 19th century, fashionable music, pictures, and stories were more about feelings and imagination than real life. This artistic trend was known as Romanticism. Because these characters inhabit both the real world and an ideal, imaginary one, *Giselle* represents Romanticism perfectly.

25

Giselle
The betrayal

HILARION EMERGED FROM LOYS' COTTAGE, frowning and confused. He was holding a velvet cloak and a silver sword. What did they mean?

Before he could decide, a trumpet flourish forced him into hiding. A duke and an elegant countess, Bathilde, swept into the clearing, with a splendid party of noblemen and ladies close behind.

Everyone came running to peer at the courtly nobles. Awed by their embroidered clothes and golden jewels, Giselle and her mother curtsied low and offered the visitors a refreshing drink.

"Tell me, dear" said Bathilde, "what do you do all day?"

"I love to dance," Giselle admitted, skipping shyly through a few steps.

"Are you in love too?" asked Bathilde.

ALICIA MARKOVA (1910-2004)
Born Lilian Alicia Marks, Markova was the first British ballerina to take the role of Giselle. She became a professional dancer at 14, performed all over the world, and was one of the founders of the company that is now English National Ballet.

HARVEST WALTZ
Most ballets contain colourful dances for the ensemble – here, the Pennsylvania Ballet – that decorate the action but do not convey information.

Giselle poses for her friends as they crown her Queen of the Vineyard.

Bathilde is charmed by Giselle's admiration.

Giselle has never seen such a splendid gown.

Hot and tired after his long walk, the duke relaxes in the shade.

The visitors enjoy the cool drinks Giselle and her mother have provided.

"Yes," smiled Giselle, but when she could not spot Loys among her friends, she entertained Bathilde by herself, leaping and spinning gaily.

Praising her graceful performance, the guests withdrew for a rest. Just then Loys returned to the clearing, and as Giselle began to describe her encounter, Hilarion thrust the sword between them.

"Ask Loys about this," he demanded. "He is not a peasant at all."

"I do not believe you," said Giselle, shaking her head.

"Look at the crest," Hilarion insisted. He held the sword beside a hunting horn left hanging on a nail, and their crests matched perfectly. Then he blew the horn, and the nobles answered its call at once.

"Count Albrecht," exclaimed Bathilde. "What are you doing here?"

Loys tried to pretend his disguise was a joke, but Giselle understood the truth. "Leave him alone," she cried, "he is going to marry me".

"No," Bathilde retorted, "he is going to marry me".

Giselle's mind suddenly snapped. Heartbroken and mad with grief, she lurched from Loys to Hilarion to her mother, recognizing no one. Finally, with a great gasp, she collapsed and died.

STEP: DÉVELOPPÉ
The Bolshoi Ballet's Svetlana Lunkina performs this movement during Giselle's dance with her friends. *Développé* means unfold: the dancer draws one pointed foot up her supporting leg, then gradually unfolds it (to the front, side, or back) until it is straight.

Giselle's madness horrifies her friends, but they cannot calm her.

Deeply ashamed, Loys turns his face away as Hilarion reveals his secret to Giselle.

Blinded by tears, the crazed girl stumbles when she tries to dance.

In her madness, Giselle believes the sword is a wriggling snake.

MAD MEMORIES
During the mad scene, Giselle conveys her confusion and sorrow with her face and broken gestures, only sketching steps she danced with Loys earlier. Here, the Spanish dancer Alicia Amatriain of the Stuttgart Ballet takes on this great dramatic challenge.

Giselle
The realm of the Wilis

SEVERAL NIGHTS LATER, Hilarion ventured into the woods to visit Giselle's grave. Dampness chilled him to the bone, and ghostly creatures flitted past him like huge moths. Terrified, he ran deeper into the forest to avoid them.

As midnight struck, a regal figure emerged from the shimmering shadows. Myrtha, Queen of the Wilis, circled her dark, cold realm and then, whisking her wand overhead, summoned her subjects, who instantly surrounded her in a cloud of wings and gossamer gowns.

THE FIRST GISELLE
Giselle was created for Carlotta Grisi (1819-99), one of the finest dancers of her time. Théophile Gautier, the French poet who wrote the ballet's story, claimed that her grace and beauty inspired him.

SPELLBOUND SPIRITS
In some versions of *Giselle*, (this is The Royal Ballet), the Wilis appear draped in ghostly bridal veils, which they remove before the dancing begins. The terrifying behaviour of these mythical maidens gave rise to the expression, "It gives me the willies".

Giselle bows humbly to her haughty queen.

Myrtha, Queen of the Wilis, welcomes Giselle to the spirit world.

The Wilis were the spirits of girls who loved dancing and had died before their wedding day. Every night they rose from their graves, hoping to find a partner who would dance with them until dawn.

Veiled and pale as moonlight, Giselle stepped from their midst and whirled into her first dance with her new sisters. When the crackle of twigs announced a visitor, they darted into the shadows. Albrecht approached Giselle's grave, then knelt beside it and covered it with lilies and tears, knowing his lies had destroyed her.

"Now I will never see her again," he wept, yet suddenly there she was, right beside him, like a statue carved out of flowing mist. Torn between joy and fear, he tried to embrace her, but his hands grabbed empty air. As she drifted through the trees, Albrecht ran after her with outstretched arms. The forest closed around them, but it could not protect Hilarion, who had stumbled among the Wilis. Obeying Myrtha's command, he danced until exhaustion overcame him. Too dizzy to see, he plunged to his death in the icy pond.

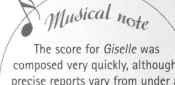

Musical note

The score for *Giselle* was composed very quickly, although precise reports vary from under a week to three weeks. At the time, the composer Adolphe Adam remarked, "This isn't work – it's play".

Long tutus like those worn by Giselle and the Wilis are called Romantic tutus.

DELICATE STRENGTH

After years of training and practice, ballerinas like Darcey Bussell develop powerful muscles. Their strength allows them to skim across the stage looking wispy and weightless. Portraying spirits, their feet seem hardly to touch the ground.

Like a vision, Giselle remains just out of Albrecht's reach.

Cold, pale, and silent, the Wilis gather at midnight to seek dancing partners.

SCENIC ILLUSION

In the 19th century, mirror panels were sometimes laid behind the dancing area to evoke the icy pond that claims Hilarion's life. In one production, the mirrors were carefully tilted so the Wilis' reflection was clearly visible.

Giselle

The triumph of love

As the waters closed over Hilarion's head, the Wilis found their next partner. Sensing the danger, Albrecht approached Myrtha with caution and respect. As she spoke, Giselle flew past like thistledown in the wind and placed herself between him and her fierce queen.

Her body told Albrecht what he must do. "Stand by the cross on my grave," it seemed to say. "You will be safe there." With a gentle nod, she guided him out of Myrtha's reach.

The queen did not expect such resistance, but her power could not touch Albrecht while the cross and Giselle's love protected him. She ordered Giselle to dance alone, luring her away from Albrecht, and Giselle could not refuse.

FOREST PHANTOMS
According to ancient legend, Wilis are young girls who were abandoned by the men they planned to marry. In death, they become angry spirits who look for revenge each night. Here, the Wilis are portrayed by the corps de ballet of Birmingham Royal Ballet.

REIGN OF TERROR
Wearing her glittering crown, Myrtha (The Royal Ballet's Jamie Tapper) inspires fear in her Wilis and her victims alike.

The Wilis surround Albrecht, who takes refuge behind Giselle.

Albrecht realized he was in danger, but his love for Giselle drew him to her side. Folding his arms around her, he danced with her all night, and as long as they remained together, nothing could harm him.

The moon sailed across the black sky during their silent dance, and starlight frosted the forest floor. Albrecht grew more tired and frightened as each hour passed. "Please let me go," he begged Myrtha and the Wilis, but thcy all turned their back.

Giselle never abandoned him. Every time he stumbled, she danced in his place, giving him time to recover his strength. ⭐ All at once, sunlight soft as gold dust powdered the treetops. The night was over, and Giselle's love had kept Albrecht alive. The Wilis and Giselle melted into the morning mist. But she remained in Albrecht's memory and in his hands, where she left a rosebud as a farewell kiss.

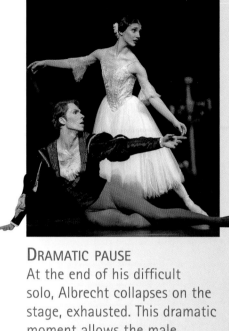

DRAMATIC PAUSE
At the end of his difficult solo, Albrecht collapses on the stage, exhausted. This dramatic moment allows the male dancer (here, The Royal Ballet's Johan Kobborg) to catch his breath while the audience applauds. The Giselle in this performance is Alina Cojocaru.

Myrtha uses this mime gesture to condemn Albrecht to death.

MIME: DIE
To express die, the dancer's arms open and the hands form tight fists. The forearms then cross in front of the body and drop with a swift, forceful jerk.

Giselle touches Albrecht for the last time before she returns to her grave.

Thanks to Giselle, Albrecht has survived, but he will never see her again.

Giselle leaves Albrecht a wild rosebud as a keepsake.

Coppélia

THE TALE OF COPPÉLIA was written by Charles Nuitter and Arthur Saint-Léon, from a story by E.T.A. Hoffmann. The comic ballet in three acts was choreographed by Saint-Léon; Léo Delibes composed the music. The first performance took place at the Opéra in Paris in 1870. Many companies still dance Coppélia today, and most productions are based on the version choreographed by Marius Petipa in 1884 and later revised by Enrico Cecchetti.

Coppélia
The lovers quarrel

IN A VILLAGE near a distant mountain peak lived an inventor named Dr Coppélius and his daughter, Coppélia. Every day Coppélia sat on her balcony reading a book, but she never moved or said a word. Even Swanilda, the friendliest girl in the village, could not make her speak.

One morning, Swanilda skipped into the square, looking for her boyfriend, Franz. She was amazed to find him grinning up at Coppélia and throwing her kisses like confetti.

"Flirts make terrible husbands," Swanilda blurted out, startling Franz with her words. ⭐ Before he could explain himself, their friends crowded around them, chattering about a new bell in the village.

"It will ring tomorrow for all new brides," the burgomaster told Swanilda. "Will you be one of them?"

Unable to hide her tears, Swanilda shook her head sadly and dashed away, leaving Franz to shrug his shoulders in innocent confusion.

SHOOTING STAR
In this Royal Ballet staging, Franz (Stuart Cassidy) tries to catch Coppélia's eye, while Swanilda (Marienela Nuñez) pouts. The first Swanilda, Giuseppina Bozzacchi, was only 16 when she created the role. She fell ill a few months after the first performance, and died on her 17th birthday.

Franz's obvious flirting is wasted on Coppélia.

MIME: FLIRT
To express flirting in mime, dancers kiss the back of their own hands quickly, one after the other.

Swanilda is annoyed by Franz's behaviour.

Franz thinks he is alone when he tries to coax a smile from Coppélia.

That evening, when Dr Coppélius left his mysterious tinkering and scurried outside for a stroll, several boys jumped from the shadows to frighten him, just for fun. The old man whacked them with his cane and finally chased them off. Hearing the commotion Swanilda and her friends rushed into the square, but by then everyone had disappeared.

Something bright in the dust caught Swanilda's eye. It was Dr Coppélius' house key, which he had dropped in the scuffle.

"What luck," she cried. "Now we can meet Coppélia face to face."

"Oh, no," wailed the girls, hanging back. "Go in there? By ourselves? Absolutely not!"

"Then I will go alone," Swanilda laughed.

Shamed by her courage, her friends swallowed their fear and tiptoed after her. Just as they vanished, Franz sneaked into the moonlit square carrying a ladder. He had made his own plans, and was going to visit Coppélia too.

FOLK DANCING
Coppélia brought the *czardas*, a lively Hungarian folk dance, to European ballet for the first time. Later, choreographers introduced many other national and traditional dances to the stage. Here, Lucy Balfour and Mikhael Plain perform with the Royal New Zealand Ballet.

The girls slip into Dr Coppélius' house.

Franz nears the house just as the girls disappear inside.

The villagers stamp and whirl in the bright sun.

SAUCY SOUBRETTE
Swanilda is the ideal role for a *soubrette* – a dancer with high spirits, bubbly charm, and a lively talent for comic acting. This is Rachel Peppin of Birmingham Royal Ballet.

35

Coppélia
In the workshop

Too FRIGHTENED even to whisper, the girls crept nervously into Dr Coppélius' workshop. They saw folded arms, glassy eyes, and crumpled bodies, all as still as stones. Pulling back a dusty curtain, Swanilda discovered Coppélia, sitting in her usual chair, reading her usual book.

"Hello," she said politely, but of course she got no answer.

She moved closer. "Has the cat got your tongue?" she asked. Again, no answer. So she reached out and tugged Coppélia's skirt. Still nothing happened.

Inching even closer Swanilda stared straight into her rival's face and dissolved into giggles. "She will never answer us," she announced to her quaking friends, "because she is a doll! They are all dolls!"

Whooping with delight, the girls wound up the toys and danced among them, causing havoc in the workshop.

WORK IN PROGRESS
In this production of *Coppélia* (Ballet du Capitole de Toulouse), dolls in various stages of construction inhabit the workshop. Here, Minh Pham is the Chinese doll, Vanessa Bonabal is the Spanish doll, Valérie Négrier is the Scottish doll, and Juan Polo is the Astrologer.

Coppélia does not look at Swanilda or move a muscle.

Swanilda pulls back the curtain and finds her rival.

36

They made so much noise that Dr Coppélius appeared in their midst without being noticed.

"Get out, all of you," he bellowed, swinging his cane at their legs as they sprinted away. Swanilda knew she could not escape, so when his back was turned she ducked behind the curtain hiding Coppélia.

Alone at last, Dr Coppélius was still patting the dolls into place when Franz slipped into the workshop from the balcony and began to explore. The old man could hardly believe it. "Why am I cursed with so much trouble?" he wondered, but now he was ready for intruders.

"What do you want?" he barked, seizing Franz by the arm.

"I... I want to marry your daughter," Franz spluttered.

Dr Coppélius smiled warmly but his eyes were cold as ice. A brilliant idea flared in his mind like a candle.

"Have a drink with me," he murmured, "and then we will discuss it like friends". He pushed Franz into a chair and filled his glass again and again, first mixing the wine with a magic potion. When Franz fell asleep, Dr Coppélius rolled up his sleeves and went to work.

LIVING DOLLS
To be convincing as dolls, dancers must have the discipline to remain still for long periods without drawing attention to themselves. Then, when they do move, their actions are a complete surprise to the audience.

The figures dangling from the rafters sway gently in the dark.

Spanish doll

Dr Coppélius chases his visitors away.

Scottish doll

When you wind him up, the clown on this mechanical bank tumbles around his cast-iron ball.

TOYS THAT MOVE
At the time *Coppélia* was created, mechanical dolls called automata were very fashionable. Although the ballet doesn't include dolls that actually come to life, it does play with the idea of realistic toys that move like people.

37

The fingers remain soft and the palms turn down.

MIME: NO

To communicate no, the dancer's hands cross at the wrist, open, then cross again. Finally, they open firmly as if brushing aside all argument. This gesture can be forceful or gentle.

IMPOSSIBLE DREAM

To bring his doll to life, Dr Coppélius employs sorcery. In some stagings – like this one by the Ballet Ensemble of Texas – he uses magic dust. Diana Herrera plays Swanilda and Keith Duncan is the toymaker.

Coppélia
Wishes come true

PULLING COPPÉLIA'S CHAIR into the centre of the room, Dr Coppélius gazed at her proudly. She was the most beautiful doll he had ever made, and now he was going to bring her to life.

He consulted the diagrams in his magic books and mumbled some ancient spells. Then he drew the energy from Franz's eyes, muscles, and bones, and thrust it towards Coppélia. First her eyes blinked. Then her shoulders wiggled. After that, she stood up and took a few stiff steps.

Dr Coppélius fell back in amazement, watching his doll move and turn by herself, and his hopes rose even higher. Concentrating with all his might, he dragged his hands across Franz's chest, absorbing the beat of his heart and guiding it into Coppélia.

A tiny smile curved her lips and she started to breathe. Dr Coppélius trembled with joy as he laid his ear against her chest and listened to her heartbeat.

"Of course my heart is beating," Swanilda was thinking. "I am a real live person. Any fool could see that."

Keeping her arms and legs rigid, Swanilda stares straight ahead.

The book of magic spells

Dr Coppélius cannot believe his eyes when the doll starts to move.

Dr Coppélius was not a fool, but his love for his creation blinded him to the truth. He did not realize Swanilda was pretending to be Coppélia, so the faster she danced, the happier he became.

Swanilda grew tired of her disguise when she noticed Franz, snoring at the table. While she tried to wake him, she set all the dolls in motion, hoping her mischief would distract Dr Coppélius.

"Be a good girl, please," the old man protested, stumbling after her to undo the damage, but Swanilda ignored him. Yanking Franz to his feet she shoved him out the door, and they ran away together.

Left alone, poor Dr Coppélius collapsed in despair. Beside him flopped the twisted body of his dear Coppélia, who had never really come to life at all.

ALEXANDRA DANILOVA (1903–1997)

This well-loved Russian ballerina danced Swanilda when she was a student. Here, she takes the role with the Sadler's Wells (later Royal) Ballet during the 1940s. In 1974, Danilova staged her own production of *Coppélia* for New York City Ballet.

Dr Coppélius fears that Coppélia will never be as good as new.

Swanilda dances a jig, wearing the Scottish doll's tartan sash.

Overcome by the drugged wine, Franz sees and hears nothing.

Dr Coppélius' work trunk overflows with hats, buttons, and ribbons.

SWITCHING ROLES

When *Coppélia* was created, male dancers appeared only to carry women. For many years, therefore, Franz was danced by a woman dressed as a man. The Paris Opéra continued this custom until the 1950s. In ballet, women who play men's roles and men who take women's parts are said to be performing *en travesti*.

Coppélia
A day to celebrate

MORNING BELLS
The composer, planned the final act of *Coppélia* as a Festival of Bells, and he wrote music for all the occasions when the new bell would ring: dawn, prayer, work, war, marriage and the hours of the day. Here, The Royal Ballet corps de ballet perform Morning hours.

Bright and early the next morning, all the villagers assembled on the rolling lawn of the manor house. ⭐ The lord of the manor had promised the village a new bell and invited everyone to celebrate its arrival from the foundry.

Trellises of flowers caught the sunlight in a net of many colours, and crisp banners flapped in the breeze. All the young couples received a blessing and a small dowry from the generous lord.

With their arms entwined, Swanilda and Franz led the parade of contented brides and grooms. But as the Burgomaster was thanking the local lord for the bell, a gloomy shadow fell across the lawn.

Dr Coppélius had wrapped Coppélia in a blanket and brought her along from the workshop. He was furious. "I want an explanation," he grumbled, pointing to the ruined doll. "I want an apology. I must be paid for the damage. I demand justice."

CHOOSE YOUR ENDING
In some productions, Dr Coppélius cannot bring himself to share the lovers' joy, so he leaves the wedding to return to work. In others, however, he cheers up and joins the celebration. This toymaker is Craig Sanok of Ballet Jörgen, Canada.

The villagers bring the bright bell to church.

Coppélia hangs limply in her maker's arms.

Dr Coppélius is already imagining new ways to bring his dolls to life.

A bag of gold helps lift Dr Coppélius' spirits.

Swanilda and Franz begged him to forgive them for their prank. "Please take my dowry," said Swanilda. "It is not much, but maybe it will be enough to repay you for the trouble we caused. We never meant to harm you with our tricks."

She smiled so sweetly and spoke so sincerely that Dr Coppélius forgave her at once, and when the Burgomaster handed him a bag of gold coins, his anger evaporated. Muttering gruff good wishes to Swanilda and all the pretty brides, he trotted happily back to his workshop and his faithful dolls.

Franz hugged Swanilda hard, and she hugged him back. "No more dolls for me," he promised. "A real girl is much more lively, and more fun too. I gladly give you my heart, Swanilda."

"Good," she said, with a saucy wink, "I am delighted to accept it".

BETTER LATE
Writing down, or notating, steps preserves movement that might be forgotten. The original steps for *Coppélia* were never notated, so the wedding pas de deux danced today by The Royal Ballet's Miyako Yoshida and Carlos Acosta (above) was created more than one hundred years later.

The new brides and grooms celebrate their weddings.

Swanilda feels content at last, certain that Franz will be a faithful husband.

Franz knows he has chosen the right girl.

I THEE WED
Even leading dancers often move around realistically without dance steps. Here, Swanilda and Franz (Diana Herrara and Lee Scoggins of the Ballet Ensemble of Texas) kneel to swear their love for each other.

41

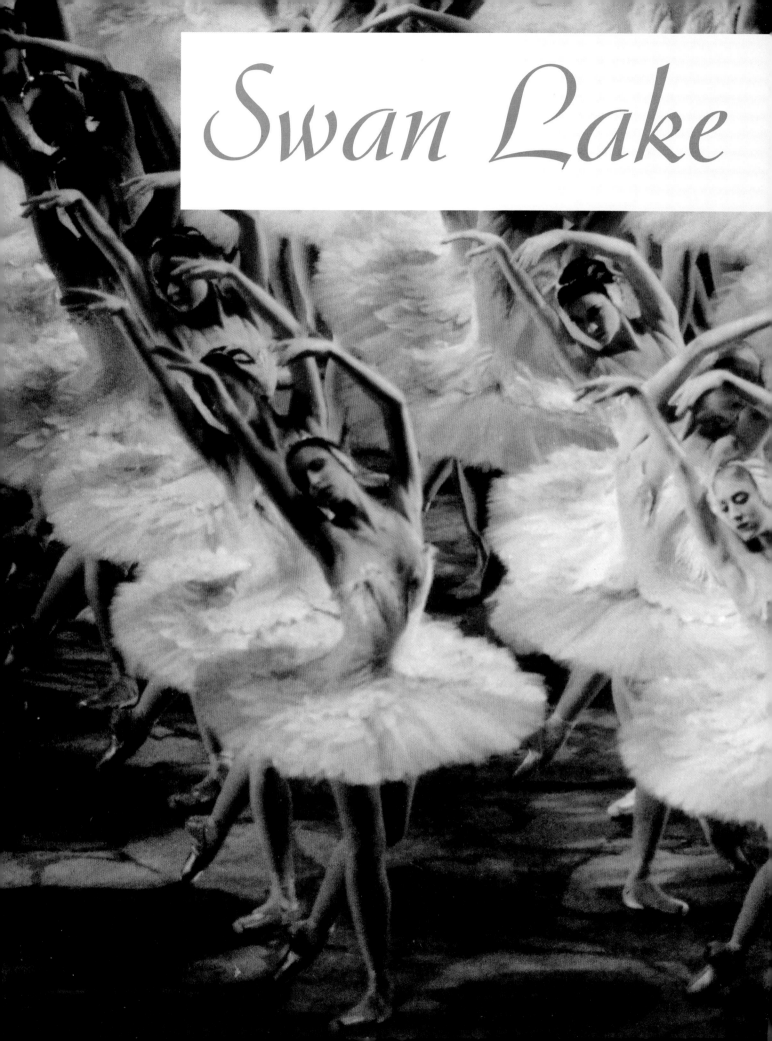

Swan Lake

THE DRAMATIC BALLET *Swan Lake*, for which Tchaikovsky composed the first of his three great ballet scores, failed when it was first staged in Moscow in 1877. Lev Ivanov and Marius Petipa then choreographed a new version, first performed in 1895 at the Maryinsky Theatre in St Petersburg and the model for most later stagings. Today *Swan Lake* is one of the most frequently performed – and probably the best-known – ballet in existence.

Swan Lake
The prince comes of age

A ROYAL ROLE
In this ballet, the queen must appear gracious and dignified. The role is usually played by a mature and experienced dancer who can convey authority with firm conviction. In this English National Ballet staging, Jane Haworth is the queen and Roman Rykin is Siegfried.

IMPORTANT DETAILS
The props or properties that dancers use onstage must be in exactly the right place at the right time. Here, Vladimir Neporozhny of the Bolshoi Ballet raises his glass as he celebrates with his friends.

HIGH IN THE MOUNTAINS of a distant land, far above the villages and farms, Prince Siegfried and his mother, the queen, lived quietly in a great stone castle. Every year, on the afternoon of the prince's birthday, they invited the local farmers and villagers and all the prince's friends from the surrounding estates to a big party.

When Siegfried reached the age of manhood, his birthday celebration was livelier than ever, and he seemed entirely happy. He laughed and joked, graciously accepting the villagers' good wishes.

Sentries watch the party from a castle tower.

Villagers raise their glasses in a toast to the prince.

Siegfried welcomes his friends to a day of celebration.

Courtiers waltz gaily beneath the castle's stone battlements.

44

Then his friend Benno pointed towards the castle. "Here comes your mother," he whispered. "Let me take your wine glass, before she sees it." Siegfried welcomed the queen warmly, and his eyes lit up when she presented him with a gleaming crossbow for a birthday present.

As he began to thank her, she interrupted him briskly. "We have serious matters to discuss," she said. "Now that you are old enough to succeed me on the throne, it is time for you to get married."

"But I am not in love," Siegfried protested with a grin.

"That is not important," the queen continued. "I have invited a number of eligible young princesses to the ball tomorrow night. Before the evening ends, you must choose your bride."

Siegfried was thunderstruck, but he bowed obediently and hid his distress until she was out of sight.

"Cheer up," said Benno. "You can still enjoy yourself today". As he spoke, a flock of swans flew across the evening sky. "Why not try your new crossbow?" Benno suggested. The powerful, wild birds captured Siegfried's attention and raised his spirits.

"A hunt is a wonderful idea," he agreed. Seizing his crossbow, he led his friends into the darkness.

A DIFFERENT LOOK
Instead of wearing traditional costumes, the male ensemble of the Royal Ballet of Flanders play the prince's friends in modified suits of real armour. These cover only half the body, but they are still incredibly heavy.

The queen uses this gesture to express her wishes to her son.

MIME: MARRY
To indicate the idea of marriage, a dancer extends both hands in front of the body and points to the base of the left ring finger with the index finger of the right hand.

The swans pass silently overhead.

Siegfried admires the crossbow the queen has given him.

45

Swan Lake
Beside the lake

⭐ **12** SIEGFRIED AND HIS FRIENDS followed the ancient, winding paths into the darkest part of the forest. When they reached the silvery lake and spied the wild swans gliding on the surface, Siegfried raised his crossbow and took aim.

At that moment, the nearest swan left the water in a flurry of beating wings and became a beautiful woman, who arched her neck proudly and preened in the moonlight. She drew back in alarm when she saw Siegfried, but he stood perfectly still so he would not frighten her.

"Who are you?" he asked in amazement.

"I am Odette, Queen of the Swans," she answered. "An evil sorcerer named Rothbart has cast a spell on me and all these swans. We can return to human form only between midnight and dawn. I beg you not to shoot us."

ANCIENT MYTH
Enchanted swans appear in the folklore of many cultures. When Tchaikovsky composed *Swan Lake*, he would probably have known Hans Christian Andersen's story *The Wild Swans* and Richard Wagner's opera *Lohengrin*, which features a swan prince. This Odette is the Bolshoi's Ekaterina Shipulina.

BABY SWANS
The difficult dance of the cygnets (little swans) lasts for only a few minutes, but audiences look forward to it. Four of the smallest dancers in the company (this the Hungarian State Opera Ballet) link hands and perform exactly the same steps in perfect unison.

Safe in Siegfried's arms, Odette feels sure she can trust him.

The swans guard Odette from Rothbart's anger.

46

"I would not harm you," Siegfried said gently. "How can I help you?"

"Rothbart's wicked spell will last forever," Odette explained, "unless someone falls in love with me, promises to marry me, and swears he will never love anyone else."

⭐13 Fascinated by her sad tale, Siegfried wrapped his arms protectively around her, and tenderness filled his heart. "I love you," he declared, "and I will always be faithful." ⭐14 Their love grew stronger as the hours passed, and the swan maidens shared their happiness.

Rothbart remained hidden in the shadows, gloating over the plight of his innocent subjects. When dawn broke, he rose up over them, with his dark wings spread, and ordered them back to the lake. Odette tried frantically to resist, but Rothbart's magic dragged her out of Siegfried's arms. In another instant she was gone, and the stunned prince was alone, gazing helplessly into the sky as the swans flew away.

STEP: ARABESQUE
To perform an arabesque, dancers stand on one leg, stretching the other one out behind them. In this position Odette resembles a swan in flight. Above, Marie Lindqvist of the Royal Swedish Ballet is Odette and Dragos Milhalcea supports her as Siegfried.

Rothbart uses his evil power to separate Odette and Siegfried.

Siegfried cannot prevent Odette from leaving.

Odette bids farewell to her new love with a gentle kiss.

THE SOUL OF EVIL
The wicked character of Rothbart never changes, but his appearance can vary dramatically from one version to another. In some, he looks like an owl or a vulture (this is English National Ballet's Paul Lewis); in others, he takes a more human form.

Swan Lake

At the ball

Musical note

Several years before Tchaikovsky wrote *Swan Lake*, he composed a short piece called *The Lake of the Swans* for his sister's children. As far as we know, however, little of this music survives in the full-length work.

THE FOLLOWING NIGHT, the palace was ablaze with candles and crammed with guests for Siegfried's birthday ball. Entertainers from Spain, Hungary, Poland, and Italy wore robes that gleamed in the firelight, and the air smelled of perfume.

Knowing they were on display, the princesses curtsied low before Siegfried and struggled to attract his interest. They admired his palace and praised the visiting performers, but he scarcely bothered to respond. Instead he escorted them through the dances and then simply walked away. He could think of nothing but his beloved Odette.

"Will you chose a bride from these lovely girls?" the queen finally demanded.

"No, I will not," said Siegfried, stubbornly defying his mother's wishes. Before she had time to apologize to the embarrassed princesses,

WICKED PAIR
Taking orders from her evil father (Paul Lewis), Odile (Altynai Asylmuratova) tricks Siegfried into believing she is Odette. English National Ballet.

DRAMATIC CONTRAST

The contrasting roles of Odette and Odile are traditionally taken by the same dancer, who must confront the challenge of playing two characters in the same performance. Although today, Odile is widely referred to as the Black Swan, for many years custom required her to wear a bright red tutu.

Odette hopes that Siegfried remembers his promise.

Siegfried holds Odile tightly, convinced she is the woman he met by the lake.

Odile captivates Siegfried with her beauty.

The princesses understand that Siegfried will never marry any of them.

a crack of thunder shook the palace walls, and two mysterious guests appeared from nowhere. One was Rothbart, transformed into a tall, stately count. The other, his daughter, Odile, had been transformed too, so that she looked like Odette.

Convinced that Odette had come to join him, Siegfried embraced Odile happily and whirled her into a rapturous dance. Odile bewitched him with her glittering beauty, so he never noticed the real Odette fluttering anxiously at the window to remind him of his promise.

At last, breathless with excitement, he announced to the astonished court that he would marry Odile. "Are you certain you love her?" murmured Rothbart. "Do you swear it?"

Siegfried raised his arm and swore his love, and the count burst into mocking laughter. "You have betrayed Odette," he cried, "and now she is mine forever." He tossed his cloak around Odile, and they vanished.

At once Siegfried realized that he had been tricked. Without a word, he raced out of the ballroom, desperate to find Odette and right the terrible wrong he had committed.

A FLASH OF DANGER
Odile and Odette perform many of the same steps, but create entirely different effects with them. Odile's approach is hard and menacing rather than soft and lyrical. This is the National Ballet of Cuba's Viengsay Valdéz and Joel Carreña.

Court musicians play to announce the royal guests.

Odile tricks Siegfried into a proposal of marriage.

No one recognizes Rothbart, the evil sorcerer.

Siegfried can hardly wait to claim his bride.

DANCING PRINCESSES
At the ball, several folk dances are staged for the guests. Usually, the princesses perform separately for Siegfried, but in this Stuttgart Ballet production, each one appears with her country's dancers. Above, as the Princess of Poland, Oihane Herrero leads the mazurka.

Swan Lake

The lovers are united

PIERINA LEGNANI (1868–1930)
Trained in Italy, this legendary Odette created the leading role when *Swan Lake* was successfully revised. To show off her spectacular technique, Legnani performed a dazzling sequence of whipping turns called fouettés, which remain in the ballet to this day.

BEVY OF SWANS
Portraying the enchanted swans, the corps de ballet (here, from American Ballet Theater) enhance the ethereal atmosphere of the lakeside scenes and provide a fluid frame for the principal dancers.

WHEN ODETTE RETURNED to the forest alone, the swans saw glistening tears on her cheeks. "I have failed you," she told them. "Siegfried has broken his promise and betrayed me. Now we have little hope of escaping from Rothbart's spell."

The swans flocked to console her, but her sorrow increased as the night wore on and Siegfried did not appear. "Be patient," the swans urged. "He will come to you as soon as he recognizes his mistake."

Odette was in despair. "I cannot live like this forever," she sobbed. "I would rather die."

Suddenly a violent storm whipped across the lake, blowing her fearful words away. As the swans huddled together in the wind, trying to calm Odette, Siegfried dashed into their midst and threw himself at her feet.

Happy to be together again, Odette and Siegfried dance before the dawn breaks.

"Please forgive me," he said. "I never forgot you and I never loved anyone else. Rothbart tricked me."

Odette embraced him joyfully and forgave him with all her heart. In the peaceful hush after the storm, the lovers agreed never to part again.

"You are still mine," roared Rothbart, swooping down on them from the darkness, "and I will not release you." He snatched Odette from Siegfried's grasp and attacked the prince directly. Siegfried fought him fiercely, shielding Odette as he battled for her freedom.

When Rothbart stumbled and fell, Odette seized her chance. Kissing Siegfried one last time, she climbed the rocks and threw herself into the lake, choosing death over everlasting enchantment. Siegfried could not bear to lose her a second time. With a mighty effort, he flung Rothbart aside and hurled himself into the lake after Odette.

At last they were united, and the overwhelming power of their love defeated Rothbart and destroyed his magic. Shrieking hideously, he collapsed in a heap of feathers as the swan maidens emerged from their spell into the new day.

POWERFUL LIMBS

Rippling arms that seem to beat like wings enhance the illusion that women have become birds. All the swans (this is Keiko Amenori of Northern Ballet Theatre) must give this impression while using their arms to help them turn and balance.

Rothbart's evil power begins to fade.

THE FINAL EFFORT

In the closing moments of Swan Lake, Siegfried and Rothbart fight violently for Odette. The dancers portraying them must make the battle convincing without actually inflicting injury on one another.

Siegfried tries to protect Odette from Rothbart's fury.

Odette's love for Siegfried overcomes her fear of Rothbart.

The *Nutcracker*

$\mathcal{T}$HIS DELECTABLE BALLET was choreographed by Lev Ivanov to music by Tchaikovsky. Marius Petipa wrote the story, which he based on a German tale "The Nutcracker and the Mouse King," by E.T.A. Hoffmann. The first performance took place at the Maryinsky Theatre in St Petersburg on 18 December 1892, and the ballet has been reimagined many times since then – for modern dance troupes, tap-dancing chorus lines and ice skaters as well as traditional ballet companies.

The Nutcracker
Christmas Eve

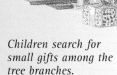

ALWAYS THE SAME GIRL
In some productions of *The Nutcracker*, the heroine is called by a Russian name, Masha. In the original story, she is Marie. Here, as Clara, the name commonly used today, The Royal Ballet's Iohna Loots accepts her present with surprised delight.

CHILDREN'S WORLD

Because so many children take parts in *The Nutcracker*, young audiences view it with special affection. The student dancers who play party guests often reappear as mice, soldiers, and sweets.

☆15 ONE FROSTY CHRISTMAS EVE many years ago, a family by the name of Stahlbaum gave a big, festive party. Clara and her little brother Fritz were so excited they could hardly wait for it to begin. ☆16 When the guests finally arrived, all the children raced into the drawing room ahead of their parents to see the candlelit tree and examine the shiny packages nestled beneath its branches.

"Your godfather is here," called Clara's mother over the hubbub of chattering and laughter. Clara ran over to greet Herr Drosselmeyer. Although he was old and quite strange, she liked him very much.

"This is my nephew," Drosselmeyer announced, nudging the boy forward to shake Clara's hand. "I have also brought your Christmas presents."

Children search for small gifts among the tree branches.

A box of toy soldiers stands at the foot of the Christmas tree.

The performing dolls are named Harlequin and Columbine.

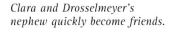
Clara and Drosselmeyer's nephew quickly become friends.

Turning some hidden keys, he set three mechanical dolls twirling like real people. Eyes wide with amazement, the children fell silent to watch them dance before the precious toys were whisked away for safekeeping.

"Now I have a special gift for a special girl," said Drosselmeyer. He drew a painted wooden soldier out of his deep pocket and showed Clara how to crack nuts with it. "What a wonderful nutcracker," Clara exclaimed. "Thank you. This is the best present of all."

"Give it to me," shouted Fritz, jealously pushing the other children aside. As he grabbed the nutcracker from Clara, it slipped through his fingers and broke on the floor.

Before Clara could cry, Drosselmeyer bandaged the nutcracker's head with his handkerchief. "He will be fine by morning," he promised Clara, who was tucking the wounded toy into one of her doll's beds. "Sleep well and do not worry."

Clutching their own presents tightly, the tired children reluctantly took their parents' hands and went home. Fritz was sent straight to his room in disgrace, and Clara kissed her nutcracker gently and went to bed too.

SNAZZY SORCERER
The Mark Morris Dance Group set *The Nutcracker* in the 1960s and renamed it *The Hard Nut.* In this unusual setting, Drosselmeyer performs only good deeds and makes wonderful things happen, as in every other production.

Stiff legs echo the action of a nutcracker – a wooden or metal tool for cracking nuts.

CREAKY JOINTS
When the nutcracker turns into a lifesize soldier, his first movements are stiff and jerky to indicate that his body is made of wood. For the Atlanta Ballet, the role is danced by Chen Xiao (above).

Clara puts her injured nutcracker to bed.

The wooden nutcracker

The adults dance while the children play.

Drosselmeyer surprises Clara with a gift chosen just for her.

THE HOUSE WAS DARK and quiet when Clara tiptoed downstairs to make sure her nutcracker was safe. To her relief, he was exactly where she had left him, but the familiar room was mysteriously different. Long shadows slid across the floor, and the midnight chime of the grandfather clock echoed eerily.

All of a sudden the Christmas tree started to sway. Its fragile ornaments trembled, the tinsel shook, and slowly the tree grew taller and taller until the top brushed the ceiling. Dwarfed by the heavy branches, Clara shivered with fright as the tree became a looming tower of winking lights.

"I must go back to bed," she thought. Turning quickly, she saw a huge, angry mouse blocking her path, and more mice, with grasping paws and lashing tails, creeping towards her from all directions.

COSTUME AND CHARACTER
Although the *Nutcracker* mice usually seem threatening and sinister, the costumes they wear in the Royal Winnipeg Ballet production turn their antics into lively cartoons.

Clara has no chance to run and hide.

An army of squealing mice follows the king into battle.

The Mouse King threatens the soldiers with his sharp claws.

Toy soldiers draw their swords to defend Clara.

"Somebody help me," she cried frantically.

At once, Fritz's tin soldiers rushed to defend her. Then the Nutcracker leaped to his feet and charged into the battle, swinging his sword at the Mouse King.

Although he fought bravely, the Nutcracker soon stumbled under the king's ferocious attack. Desperate to save him, Clara took off her slipper and hurled it straight at the Mouse King. The startled king froze, and in that instant the Nutcracker killed him with a thrust of his sword.

The defeated mice slunk away, dragging their dead king after them. The Nutcracker vanished too, and Drosselmeyer's nephew appeared in his place, dressed as a prince. Placing the Mouse King's crown on Clara's head, he led her away into a whirlwind of glistening snow.

DANCE OF THE SNOWFLAKES
Spinning and sliding steps and pointed patterns give this scene its wintry atmosphere. Here, the Birmingham Royal Ballet ensemble move so quickly, they seem to swirl like real snow. Shimmering tutus and falling "snow" glitter in the light like frost and ice.

Clara and her prince venture into the snowy night.

Clara throws her slipper at the Mouse King.

The Nutcracker springs to life and begins to fight.

LARGE AND SMALL STARS
This is the only famous ballet in which children traditionally play leading characters. Many companies, though, assign their roles to adult dancers instead. This is Jenny Tattersall in The Royal Ballet production; Ricardo Cervera is her prince.

The Nutcracker
The land of sweets

CLARA AND HER BRAVE YOUNG PRINCE emerged from the snowstorm into a fantastic land of sweets. They walked over butterscotch cobbles, past splashing fountains of lemonade and gleaming toffee pavilions, until they reached the transparent palace of the Sugar Plum Fairy.

"Thank you for coming to visit me," said the dainty fairy. Her voice rang like a cluster of silver bells. "Did you have a difficult journey?"

"We had to fight off the mice," Drosselmeyer's nephew explained. "I could not have beaten them alone, but Clara helped me by throwing her shoe at the Mouse King. Together we won the battle." Clara's face glowed with pleasure as he recounted the frightening events. She was proud of her courage, even though she did not say so.

CHINESE STYLE
For more than 200 years, the same gestures have been used to define Chinese characters in ballet. Dancers bend their elbows, curl their hands into fists, and point their index fingers up. Marta Barahona is Clara in this Royal Ballet staging.

TASTY MORSELS
The dances in this scene are known by a number of different names; instead of Coffee, Tea, Chocolate, and Peppermint, they are sometimes described as Arabian, Chinese, Spanish, and Russian. The Shepherdess dance is often called Pastoral or Dance of the mirlitons (reed pipes).

Some houses are made from toffee, chocolate, and licorice.

Clara and Drosselmeyer's nephew are the honoured guests.

Everything in the land of sweets is made of sugar and spice.

An Arabian dancer sways through the Coffee dance.

"If you would like to rest here for a while, I will invite an assortment of my sweets to dance for you," said the Sugar Plum Fairy. She escorted the children to a splendid throne, where pages no bigger than elves offered them delicious cakes and cool drinks. Then, with a flourish of her wand, she summoned the entertainers.

First Chocolate slithered out of the crowd in a fiery Spanish dance that melted stamping feet and twisting shoulders into a creamy swirl. Then the tantalizing figure of Arabian Coffee drifted by, floating in a cloud of veils as light and lacy as foam. ☆17 Chinese Tea burst into the hall like a stream of sunshine. Bubbling gaily, he bowed and bowed to the children and the other guests.

☆18 Next in the parade of entertainers came the boisterous Russian Peppermints, who tumbled head over heels past the throne, spraying slivers of energy everywhere. ☆19 A flock of Marzipan Shepherdesses added demure refinement to the procession.

JUMPING JACKS
In the original production, dancers dressed as clowns jumped through hoops in the Russian dance. Many recent stagings, however, feature vibrant peasants or soldiers instead. This one is Lee Scoggings in a Ballet Ensemble of Texas performance.

Spun-sugar icing forms the lacy arch.

Candy-cane columns

Chinese Tea leaves the floor.

The Russians leap through their hoops.

Proud Spanish dancers represent Chocolate.

The arms curve in a graceful, inviting arc.

MIME: COME
To express come, dancers lift both arms in the same direction and round them gently, keeping the elbows down and the hands turned up. Then they lower both arms and bring them close to the body.

59

The Nutcracker
The Sugar Plum Fairy

Tara Butler of the Jörgen Ballet, Canada

CLARA CLAPPED HER HANDS in glee and popped three jellybeans into her mouth. "Which dance did you like best?" she asked her prince. "Who do you think will appear next? I never knew the world could hold so much sweetness and so many surprises."

The boy smiled back at her, and she noticed the iced cakes had turned his mouth so red it looked like a cherry. Before he could reply, roly-poly Mother Ginger bustled into the hall, flapping her apron and herding all her children in front of her.

Soft and smooth as a pillow, she waited patiently while they romped and skipped around her. Then she flung her arms wide and gathered them up in a loving hug.

DANCING BELLS
The Sugar Plum Fairy dances alone to one of the ballet's most enchanting melodies, played on the celeste – a keyboard instrument that sounds like tiny bells. The celeste was newly invented when Tchaikovsky wrote this score.

Popular sweets in the 19th century, sugar plums are candied fruits.

HIDDEN TREASURE
Sometimes a character called Mother Ginger, or *Mère Gigogne*, appears in huge hoop skirts. The children hiding inside burst out to dance. This is the Ballet Ensemble of Texas.

Mother Ginger glides among her frisky children, laughing merrily.

The candied flowers form a pretty posy.

Children pop out from beneath Mother Ginger's huge skirt.

They were still tickling one another and giggling with pleasure when she led them away.

In the hush they left behind them, a cascade of candied flowers danced across the glazed floor. Unfolding their gilded petals in overlapping waves, the blossoms swept through the hall, weaving intricate patterns around the candy-cane columns and finally arranging themselves in a neat bouquet.

At last the Sugar Plum Fairy reappeared, with her own handsome prince by her side. Their elegant poise and gentle grace transformed their dance into a tender private conversation. ⭐20 When the fairy danced alone, she seemed to Clara like a delicate vision, as perfect as a beautiful dream.

"I want to be just like her when I grow up," Clara thought, "and I want every party to be as lively and pretty and happy as this one". Stepping down from her throne, she kissed the Sugar Plum Fairy and thanked the entertainers. Then she took her prince's hand and they set off together to explore the future.

GRACEFUL PETALS
In this famous waltz, the dancers form intricate lines and curves to evoke fresh flowers and man-made bouquets. Here, the Royal Swedish Ballet ensemble represent the blooms.

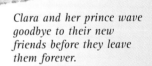

Clara and her prince wave goodbye to their new friends before they leave them forever.

HAPPY ENDINGS

Many productions of *The Nutcracker* end with Clara moving into the future, either by herself or with her handsome prince. In some versions, she wakes up in her own bed at home and realizes that her exciting adventure was only a Christmas-time dream.

The Sugar Plum Fairy scarcely touches the ground when she dances.

Glossary

Act The main divisions of the action of a ballet, separated by intervals/intermissions.

Adagio Musical term meaning at ease or leisure. Slow and smooth movements.

Air, en l' In the air. An action of the working leg off the floor.

Arabesque Pose on one straight leg with the working leg extended straight behind the body.

Assemblé Jump that brings two straight legs together in the air before landing in fifth position.

Attitude Pose on one straight leg with the working leg bent to the front or back.

Ballerina From the Italian ballare, meaning to dance. The highest rank of female dancer in a company.

Ballet Theatrical performance of group and solo dances that combine steps and music, often to tell a story.

Ballon Refers to springiness of movement and the bouncy quality of a dancer's jumps.

Barre Railing (wall-fixed or freestanding) that dancers use for support in the opening exercises of their lessons.

Battement, grand Large beating. A high kick of the straight leg to the front, side or back.

Czardas in Coppélia

Battement, tendu Stretched beating. The working leg slides open to the front, side, or back – with the toes resting lightly on the floor – and then closes again.

Beat To strike the legs together in the air before completing a jump.

Bolero Lively Spanish dance in triple time, often accompanied by castanets.

Bourrée A series of small, even running steps in fifth position, performed quickly and lightly. The front foot advances, and the back foot catches up with it.

Bras Arm or arms.

Cabriole Jump where one leg kicks up, to the front, side, or back, and the other rises to meet it in the air.

Caractère Character. Describes roles that require acting and mime gestures but few classical steps.

Centre work The second part of a ballet class, after the barre exercises, in which the dancers work in the centre of the room without support.

Changement Jump from fifth position to fifth position, in which the feet change place in the air.

Choreographer The person who chooses and arranges the steps of a ballet.

Choreography The arrangement of steps in a ballet.

Classical ballet Work based on the traditional technique that developed from 17th-century court dancing.

Corps de ballet Body of the ballet. The dancers in a company, often the youngest, who perform as a group, framing the solo dancers and enhancing the atmosphere.

Czardas A lively Hungarian folk dance. There is Czardas music in both *Swan Lake* and *Coppélia*.

Danseur Male dancer.

Danseur, premier First dancer. The leading male dancer.

Décor The scenery and costumes for a ballet.

Demi Half. A small position.

Développé Developing movement in which the working leg unfolds gradually after it leaves the floor until it is straight at its highest point.

Divertissement Diversion. The dances that show off the dancers' skill and grace without advancing the story.

Échappé Escape. A move where the feet begin in a closed position, spring open, and stay apart.

Elevation Refers to a dancer's ability to jump high.

Ensemble Together. The entire company or the corps de ballet as a unit.

Entrechat Jump that begins and ends in fifth position, with the feet crisscrossing several times in the air.

Épaulement The graceful placing of the head, neck, and shoulders.

Fermé Closed. A movement that ends with the feet together.

Flies The area high above the stage in which huge backcloths, painted as scenery, are stored until they are needed.

Flying The raising of scenery above the stage. Also, the movement of dancers through the air on wires.

Folk dancing Native dances of any country used as part of a ballet.

Glissade Gliding step, done in any direction.

Grand Big. A big movement.

Grand pas de deux An important dance for the ballerina and her partner. It usually contains a slow duet (adagio), then solos (variations) for each dancer, and a rapid closing duet (called the coda).

Jambe Leg.
Jambe, rond de Circular leg movement, either on the ground or in the air.
Jeté Thrown. A jump from one foot to the other.
Jeté, grand Big jump that throws the body through the air.
Jeté, petit Small jump that quickly shifts the weight from one foot to the other.

Leotard Skintight garment, with or without sleeves and legs, worn for class and rehearsals.
Line The straight line or curve formed by a dancer's body.

Mark To sketch or indicate a movement in class or rehearsal.
Matinée An afternoon performance.
Mazurka Polish folk dance with three strong beats, marked by foot-stamping and heel-clicking.
Mime The use of arm and hand gestures to represent words. The gestures follow the order of words in a French sentence.

Notation Writing down movement in symbols rather than words.

Ouvert Open. A movement that ends with the feet apart.
Overture Music played before the curtain rises and the first dancers appear.

Pas Step.
Pas de chat Step of the cat. A light high jump in which one foot after the other is pulled close to the body.
Pas de deux Dance for two.

Pas de trois Dance for three.
Pas de quatre Dance for four.
Petit Small. A small movement.
Pirouette One or more turns on the spot with the working foot pointing to the knee of the supporting leg.
Plié Bending. Where one or both knees bend over the toes.
Pointe shoe Woman's shoe with a stiffened toe on which the dancer stands. Also called a toe shoe.
Port de bras The carriage of the arms. The placing of the arms in relation to the head and body.
Prologue Introduction to the main action. The first act of *The Sleeping Beauty* is called the Prologue.

Relevé Raised. Raising the body by lifting the heels off the floor.
Romantic ballet Works created in the 19th century that contrast reality with fantasy.
Rosin A powder dancers use on their shoes to stop them from slipping in class or performance.

Saut Jump from two feet that ends with the feet in the original position.
Sauté Jumped. Any movement to which a hop is added.
Scene Short portion of an act, marked by the appearance of additional characters or by a change of location.
Scenery The furniture and backgrounds that establish the action's time and place.
Solo Dance for one.
Soubrette Spirited female dancer with bubbly charm and a talent for comic acting.
Spotting The practice of focusing on a distant object while turning, then whipping the head back around to it to avoid getting dizzy.
Stage left To the left, from a position on the stage facing the audience.

Stage right To the right, from a position on the stage facing the audience.
Supporting leg The leg supporting the body's weight while the other leg is off the floor.

Tendu Stretched. *See* Battement, tendu.
Terre, à On the ground. An action of the working leg on the floor.
Terre à terre Ground to ground. Steps that leave the floor only briefly, as opposed to jumps.
Tour A turn of the body.
Tour en l'air Complete turn of the body in the air.
Travesti, en Refers to a female playing the part of a man, or the other way around.
Turnout Basic aspect of classical dance in which the legs turn away from each other at all times.
Tutu, classical Woman's costume, tightly fitted around the body and waist, with a stiff frill for the skirt.
Tutu, Romantic Woman's costume, tightly fitted around the body, with a calf-length, gauzy skirt.

Variation Solo dance.

Waltz Dance in triple time or based on the count of three.
Working leg Leg that moves while the other leg supports the body.

Swan Lake pas de deux

Index

Acknowledgments

The publishers would like to thank the following: Michael Johnstone for advice on music; Porselli Dance Wear in Covent Garden, London, for the loan of leotards and tights; Dr Giannandrea Poesio for guidance with mime gestures; Margaret Barbieri from the London Studio Centre, and students Amy Bailey, Anthony Gordon, Michelle McGuire and Juan Rodriguez; Darryl Jaffray, The Royal Opera House, Katie Town, The Royal Ballet, and The Royal Ballet School staff for help and information; Royal Academy of Dancing library; Kay Ollerenshaw for the index; Paul Dawson and Patch McQuaid for work on the CD.

The publisher would also like to thank the following for their kind permission to reproduce their photographs:
(Key: a-above; c-centre; b-below; l-left; r-right; t-top)
Myra Armstrong: American Ballet Theatre 42-43, 50bl. Atlanta Ballet: Kim Kenney 55cr.

Ballet du Capitole de Toulouse: STC Patrice Nin 21tr, 36cl. www.bridgeman.co.uk: Walter Hussey Bequest, Pallant House, Chichester, UK 16tl; Bibliotheque de L'Opéra, Paris, France/ Archives Charmet; 28tl. Dee Conway: Bolshoi Ballet 27tr; English National Ballet 47br; Kirov Ballet 10-11, 17tr, 20tl; Northern Ballet Theatre 51tr; The Royal Ballet 7bl, 18cl, 30cl, 31tr, 41tr, 57br, 58tl. Bill Cooper: Birmingham Royal Ballet 35cr. Corbis: Robbie Jack/Birmingham Royal Ballet 30tl. Anthony Crickmay: 7tr, 7c, 29cr. DK Images: Judith Miller/Noel Barrett Antiques & Auctions Ltd 37cr. Empics Ltd: EPA/Alejandro Ernesto/Stuttgart Ballet 27cr. Getty Images: 7tl; Baron 26tl; Baron/Hulton Archive 39tr; Bruno Vincent/Bolshoi Ballet 44bl; Patrick Riviere/Australian Ballet 14tl. Hungarian State Opera: Béla Mezey 46cl. Robbie Jack Photography: The Royal Ballet 12tl, 32-33, 40tl; Kirov Ballet 13tr; Royal Ballet of Flanders 45tr. Ballet Jörgen Canada: Photographer: David Hou; 40cl; Photographer: David Hou; 60tl. Paul Kolnik: Pennsylvania Ballet 26cl. Laurent

Philippe Photographe: Les Ballet de Monte Carlo 19cr. Retna Pictures Ltd: Fernando Aceves/ National Opera of Ukraine, Kiev 15br. Reuters: Rafael Perez AB/HB National Ballet of Cuba 49tr; The Royal Ballet/Natasha-Marie Brown 22-23, 28cl. Rex Features: Reg Wilson 48cl. Linda Rich/Dance Picture Library: Birmingham Royal Ballet 52-53, 57tr; Bolshoi Ballet 46tl; The Royal Ballet 7br, 14bl, 24tl, 34tl, 54tl; Vienna Festival Ballet 21br. Royal New Zealand Ballet: Maarten Holl 2004 35tr. Royal Swedish Ballet: Alexander Kenney 47tr; Mats Bäcker 61tr. Royal Winnipeg Ballet: David Cooper 20cl, 56cl. Stuttgart Ballet: 15tr, 25tr, 49br; Theatre Museum, London: Courtesy of the Trustees of the V&A: 50tl. Topfoto.co.uk: English National Ballet/UPPA Ltd 44tl. Cathy Vanover Photography: Ballet Ensemble of Texas 36tl, 37tr, 38clb, 41br, 59tr, 60bl. © Jack Vartoogian: FrontRowPhotos/Mark Morris Dance Group 55tr.

All other images © Dorling Kindersley
For further information see: www.dkimages.com